New Man
New Tongue

New Man
New Tongue

by
John MacArthur, Jr.

MOODY PRESS
CHICAGO

All Scripture quotations, unless noted otherwise, are from the *New Scofield Reference Bible*, King James Version. Copyright © 1967 by Oxford University Press, Inc. Reprinted by permission.

Library of Congress Cataloging in Publication Data

MacArthur, John, 1939-
    New man, new tongue / by John MacArthur, Jr.
      p.   cm.   (John MacArthur's Bible studies)
    Messages delivered at Grace Community Church in Panorama City, Calif.
    Includes indexes.
    ISBN 0-8024-5365-1
    1. Bible. N.T. Colossians IV, 2-6—Criticism, interpretation, etc. 2. Bible. N.T. James III, 1-12—Criticism, interpretation, etc. I. Title. II. Series: MacArthur, John, 1939-   Bible studies.
BS2715.2.M32   1988
227'.706—dc19   87-34739
                                                      CIP

1 2 3 4 5 6 7 Printing/LC/Year 93 92 91 90 89 88

Printed in the United States of America

Contents

These Bible studies are taken from messages delivered by Pastor-Teacher John MacArthur, Jr., at Grace Community Church in Panorama City, California. The recorded messages themselves may be purchased as a series or individually. Please request the current price list by writing to:

WORD OF GRACE COMMUNICATIONS
P.O. Box 4000
Panorama City, CA 91412

Or call the following toll-free number:
1-800-55-GRACE

1

The Speech of the New Man—Part 1

Outline

Introduction
A. The Effect of Christianity on What We Say
B. The Emphasis in the Bible on What We Say
    1. The mouth of the unredeemed
    2. The mouth of the redeemed

Lesson
I. The Speech of Prayer (v. 2)
    A. "Continue in prayer"
        1. Its constancy
        2. Its consciousness
        3. Its commitment
            a) Identified
                (1) Acts 10:2
                (2) Acts 1:14
                (3) Acts 2:42
            b) Illustrated
                (1) Luke 18:1-8
                (2) Luke 11:5-10
    B. "Watch in the same"
        1. The basic meaning
        2. The broad meaning
    C. "With thanksgiving"
        1. Gratitude reflected in Colossians
        2. Gratitude reflected in us
            a) For God's presence
            b) For God's provision
            c) For God's pardon
            d) For God's promise

Introduction

In Matthew 12:34 Jesus says, "Out of the abundance of the heart the mouth speaketh." What He meant by that statement was that what we are on the inside will come out of our mouths. That is the key to the Colossians 4:2-6 passage. Basically the apostle Paul is saying, "If you're a new man in Christ, and if you're living the risen life, it's going to affect the things you say." Paul's overall thrust as he concludes the book of Colossians is that the new man is different.

Paul has been describing the life-style of the new man. In Colossians 3:5-17 Paul discusses the personal life of the new man, independent of anyone else. Second, he discusses the new man in relation to the people in his own family (3:18–4:1). Now, in Colossians 4:2, Paul discusses a third dimension: the new man in relation to those outside his family, particularly unbelievers (vv. 5-6). The emphasis in Colossians 4:2-6 is how the new man speaks in front of a watching world, which evaluates Christianity on the basis of what it hears from this "new" man.

A. The Effect of Christianity on What We Say

One of the things that happens when we become Christians is that the Lord changes the things we talk about. Many people have confessed to me, "You know, since I became a Christian I don't swear anymore. It's amazing—I talk different!" That's true because "out of the abundance of the heart the mouth speaketh." If you have a renewed heart, then you're going to have a renewed mouth.

Ephesians 4:24-29 closely parallels our text in Colossians 4:2-6. It begins, "Put on the new man, which after God is created in righteousness and true holiness." This is the same thought as in Colossians 3—put on the new man because you are a new man. How are we to do that? Starting in Ephesians 4:25, Paul deals with the mouth: "Wherefore, putting away lying, speak every man truth with his neighbor. . . . [Don't be] angry." Then in verse 29 he says, "Let no corrupt communication proceed out of your mouth, but that which is good to the use of edifying, that it may minister grace unto the hearers." Notice that immediately after he discusses the new man in verse 24, he goes into a rather

8

lengthy message relative to the mouth. Christianity should have a profound effect on the mouth. A person's speech should be greatly altered by the fact that he's been redeemed.

B. The Emphasis in the Bible on What We Say

It isn't easy to control the tongue; it's the one faculty the Bible emphasizes above every other. In James 3:3-12 James points out the tremendous power of the tongue, the damage it can do, and its inconsistency in that it can provide blessing one moment and cursing the next.

1. The mouth of the unredeemed

The mouth is perhaps the truest indicator of the spiritual condition of a person. The unredeemed mouth is the gate through which depravity exits. Isaiah, for example, when he was defining sinfulness in relation to his people, simply said, "Woe is me! For I am undone, because I am a man of unclean lips, and I dwell in the midst of a people of unclean lips" (6:5). He was simply saying that depravity is proved by conversation. In Matthew 12:37 Jesus says that men will be condemned on the basis of the words that come out of their mouths. The Bible has much to say about what the depraved mouth is like. Here is a biblical description of the unredeemed mouth and what proceeds from it.

a) Evil—"The mouth of the wicked pours out evil things" (Prov. 15:28, NASB*).

b) Lust—"For the lips of an adulteress drip honey, and smoother than oil is her speech" (Prov. 5:3, NASB).

c) Deceit—"Their tongue is a deadly arrow; it speaks deceit; with his mouth one speaks peace to his neighbor, but inwardly he sets an ambush for him" (Jer. 9:8, NASB).

d) Curses—"His mouth is full of curses" (Ps. 10:7, NASB).

*New American Standard Bible.

9

e) Oppression—"His mouth is full of . . . oppression" (Ps. 10:7, NASB).

f) Lies—"Lying lips are an abomination to the Lord" (Prov. 12:22, NASB).

g) Perversity—A wicked man "is the one who walks with a false [perverse or twisted] mouth" (Prov. 6:12, NASB).

h) Destruction—"By the blessing of the upright a city is exalted, but by the mouth of the wicked it is torn down" (Prov. 11:11, NASB). A mouth can literally destroy a city by creating political havoc, war, and so on.

i) Vanity—"For speaking out arrogant words of vanity, they entice" (2 Pet. 2:18, NASB).

j) Flattery—"A flattering mouth works ruin" (Prov. 26:28, NASB).

k) Foolishness—"The mouth of fools spouts folly" (Prov. 15:2, NASB).

l) Madness—"The lips of a fool consume him . . . and the end of it is wicked madness" (Eccles. 10:12-13, NASB).

m) Wordiness—"The fool multiplies words" (Eccles. 10:14, NASB).

n) Idle words—"Every idle word that men shall speak, they shall give account of it in the day of judgment" (Matt. 12:36).

o) False doctrine—"Empty talkers . . . teaching things they should not teach, for the sake of sordid gain" (Titus 1:10-11, NASB).

p) Wicked plots—"The wicked plots against the righteous, and gnashes at him with his teeth" (Ps. 37:12, NASB). Many times in the Bible we see the wicked using their mouths to plot against the righteous.

q) Pride—"In the mouth of the foolish is a rod of pride" (Prov. 14:3).

r) Hatred—"They have also surrounded me with words of hatred" (Ps. 109:3, NASB).

s) Swearing oaths—Jesus said, "Make no oath at all . . . . But let your statement be, 'Yes, yes' or 'No, no'; and anything beyond these is of evil" (Matt. 5:34, 37, NASB).

t) Foul language—"Let no corrupt communication proceed out of your mouth" (Eph. 4:29).

u) Gossip—"They are gossips, slanderers" (Rom. 1:29, NASB). "The words of a whisperer are like dainty morsels, and they go down into the innermost parts of the body" (Prov. 26:22, NASB).

Summing up the unregenerate mouth are Paul's words in Romans 3:13-14: "Their throat is an open sepulcher; with their tongues they have used deceit; the poison of asps is under their lips; whose mouth is full of cursing and bitterness." What is most interesting about this description is that Paul started in the throat and came out to the lips, showing the corruptness of the whole process.

2. The mouth of the redeemed

What should a redeemed mouth do?

a) Confess sin—David said, "When I kept silence, my bones became old through my roaring all the day long. . . . I acknowledged my sin unto thee, and mine iniquity have I not hidden. I said, I will confess my transgression unto the Lord, and thou forgavest the iniquity of my sin" (Ps. 32:3, 5).

b) Confess Christ—"If thou shalt confess with thy mouth the Lord Jesus . . . thou shalt be saved. . . . With the mouth confession is made unto salvation" (Rom. 10:9-10).

c) Speak good things—"Let no corrupt communication proceed out of your mouth, but that which is good to the use of edifying" (Eph. 4:29).

d) Speak God's law—"The Lord's law may be in thy mouth" (Ex. 13:9). "These words, which I commanded thee this day, shall be in thine heart; and thou shalt teach them diligently unto thy children, and shalt talk of them when thou sittest in thine house, and when thou walkest by the way, and when thou liest down, and when thou risest up" (Deut. 6:6-7).

e) Praise God—"His tongue was loosed, and he spoke, and praised God" (Luke 1:64).

f) Teach truth—God told Moses that He would be with his mouth and teach him what to do and say (Ex. 4:15).

g) Bless others—"Not rendering evil for evil, or railing for railing, but on the contrary, blessing, knowing that ye are called to this" (1 Pet. 3:9).

h) Speak of God—"I will . . . talk of Thy doings" (Ps. 77:12).

i) Speak wisdom and kindness—"She openeth her mouth with wisdom, and in her tongue is the law of kindness" (Prov. 31:26).

j) Turn away wrath—"A soft answer turneth away wrath" (Prov. 15:1).

The Bible has much to say about what we should or shouldn't say. As new creatures, then, we must be committed to the fact that a new man should have new speech.

In our text in Colossians 4:2-6 Paul discusses four kinds of speech: the speech of prayer, the speech of proclamation, the speech of performance, and the speech of perfection. Let's look at each one.

Lesson

I. THE SPEECH OF PRAYER (v. 2)

"Continue in prayer, and watch in the same with thanksgiving."

Prayer is the most important speech that your mouth will ever utter, the most important conversation that you will ever hold, the most important expression of the new life. Prayer is the divinely appointed weapon against the sinister attack of the devil and his angels; it is the vehicle for confession of sin; it is the means by which the grateful soul pours out its spontaneous praise before the throne of God; it is the voice of the weeping soul calling on the sympathetic High Priest in the time of need; it is the intercession of the concerned Christian who calls on divine resources in behalf of another's trouble; it is the simple conversation of the beloved child with the caring Father as they talk of love. Prayer is to be toward God, in line with the Holy Spirit's mind and will, and in the name of Christ. Let's look at what Paul says about prayer in verse 2.

A. "Continue in prayer"

  1. Its constancy

    a) Ephesians 6:18—"Praying always."

    b) 1 Thessalonians 5:17—"Pray without ceasing."

    c) Luke 21:36—Jesus said, "Watch ye, therefore, and pray always."

    d) Acts 6:4—The apostles gave themselves "continually to prayer."

    e) Acts 10:2—Cornelius "prayed to God always."

    f) Romans 12:12—"Continuing diligently in prayer."

    g) Philippians 4:6—"Be anxious for nothing, but in everything, by prayer and supplication."

13

2. Its consciousness

Part of the meaning of "continue in prayer" is to have God-consciousness. It doesn't mean we are to be verbally praying all the time but rather to have a general God-consciousness that sees everything that happens in reference to God. In other words, when we see something bad we pray for those involved; when we see something good we praise God, who brought it about. It's a constant flow of God-consciousness.

Although all of this is true, it doesn't capture the complete idea of continuing in prayer. Many people bail out of constant prayer by saying, "Well, it's obvious that I can't keep praying forever—God isn't deaf, and He doesn't forget what I ask Him." I believe most of us operate on that basis. We say, "Well, God, here's the need. I just wanted to remind You about it." We believe God has all the information, He's sovereign, and He's going to call the shots—so we go on to something else. That God-conscious explanation to continuance in prayer can become a way of backing out of unwanted responsibility. It isn't wrong, but it leans too heavily on one side. I want to capture what Paul is saying here from a different angle and expand it into a dimension that is rarely touched.

3. Its commitment

a) Identified

The root for the word *continue* in verse 2 is *kartereō*. It basically comes from a noun that means "strong." The verb *kartereō* means "to be steadfast, to endure, to hang in there." But the actual word used here is *proskartereō*. The Greek preposition *pros* has been added to the verb. This intensifies its meaning to mean "to be super strong, super steadfast, to hang in there." It's the idea of perseverance.

This term is used in Hebrews 11:27 to speak of Moses, who "by faith . . . forsook Egypt, not fearing the wrath of the king; for he endured, as seeing him who is invisible." He endured and stuck with it. It's a strong commitment to something—a steadfast endurance where you don't give up or quit. It is also used with that same idea throughout the book of Acts.

(1) Acts 10:2—When the text says that Cornelius "prayed to God always," it is referring to his perseverance, his strong commitment to pray.

(2) Acts 1:14—The twelve disciples in an upper room in Jerusalem "continued with one accord in prayer and supplication." That isn't referring to a general God-consciousness; they were actually involved in constant supplication for many hours and days until the Spirit of God came.

(3) Acts 2:42—The same term is used here: "They continued steadfastly in the apostles' doctrine and fellowship, and in breaking of bread, and in prayers." Here again it doesn't necessarily mean a general God-consciousness but rather a constancy in prayer—over and over, beseeching God relative to their needs.

When you delve into the term, the idea that you find is not an easy-going God-consciousness but a strong, steadfast, enduring, persevering struggle with deeply felt issues. Alexander Maclaren says that the word *proskatereō* "implies both earnestness and continuity" (*The Epistles of St. Paul to the Colossians and Philemon* [London: Hodder & Stoughton, 1906], p. 355). Kittel, who probably has the most classic commentary on the definition of Greek words, says *kartereō* means "to be strong [and] courageous" and *proskatereō* means "to pay persistent attention to . . . to hold fast to something" (*Theological Dictionary of the New Testament*, vol. 3 [Grand Rapids: Eerdmans, 1965], pp. 617-18).

b) Illustrated

(1) Luke 18:1-8—Jesus used this parable to teach the principle that "men ought always to pray, and

15

not to faint." It is the story of an unjust judge and a persistent woman, who kept coming and begging the judge to avenge her of her adversary. He refused her until finally she wearied him with her persistence and he gave her what she wanted. You may say, "Wait a minute! Do you mean that has a divine application?" Verses 6-8 say, "The Lord said, Hear what the unjust judge saith. And shall not God avenge his own elect, who cry day and night unto him, though he bear long with them? I tell you, that he will avenge them speedily." God is going to act to make things right, to gain His own honor, and to give you the place of blessing when you cry out to Him day and night (cf. Acts 20:31).

(2) Luke 11:5-10—Another story that Jesus told that illustrates this same truth is the parable of the man who had an unexpected guest in the middle of the night and had nothing to give him to eat. He went to a friend's house to borrow three loaves of bread, but the friend in effect said, "Go away and quit bugging me. The door is shut, the children are in bed with me, and I can't get up." Then Jesus said, "Though he will not rise and give him because he is his friend, yet because of his importunity he will rise and give him as many as he needeth" (v. 8). Do you know what importunity is? The man kept yelling to his friend and banging on his door. Finally his friend got out of bed because it was his only choice if he wanted to get any sleep. Jesus concluded the parable by saying, "Ask, and it shall be given you; seek and ye shall find; knock, and it shall be opened unto you" (v. 9). In other words, we are to be persistent. We are to bang away and not give up. I don't know if you think about prayer like that; but sometimes when you believe something will honor God and glorify Christ you must storm the gates of heaven. You have to struggle.

Do You Ever Wrestle with God in Prayer?

Virginia Stem Owens wrote an interesting article in *Christianity Today* ("Prayer—Into the Lion's Jaws," 19 Nov. 1976) in which she speaks of God: "This is no cosmic teddy bear we are cuddling up to. As one of the children describes Him in C. S. Lewis's *Chronicles of Narnia*, 'He's not a *tame* lion.' Jacques Ellul is convinced that prayer for persons living in the technological age must be combat, and not just combat with the Evil One, with one's society, or even one's divided self, though it is also all of these; it is combat with God. We too must struggle with Him just as Jacob did at Peniel where he earned his name *Israel*—'he who strives with God.' We too must be prepared to say, 'I will not let You go till You bless me.'

"Consider Moses, again and again intervening between the Israelites and God's wrath; Abraham praying for Sodom; the widow demanding justice of the unjust judge. But in this combat with God, Ellul cautions, we must be ready to bear the consequences: '. . . Jacob's thigh was put out of joint, and he went away lame. . . . Whoever wrestles with God in prayer puts his whole life at stake.' "

Prayer is a matter of struggling and grappling with God, proving to God the deepest concern of your heart, and pouring out to God what you believe would honor Him. We hear David in the psalms, from the deepest part of his inner being, pouring out his heart over and over again and crying to God to answer. We don't hear David saying, "O Lord, I have a request. Whatever You want will be fine, but here's my request." Prayer is to be a persistent, courageous struggle.

How Bold Are Your Prayers?

In 1540 Luther's great friend and assistant Friedrich Myconius became sick and was expected to die. On his bed he wrote a loving farewell to Luther with a trembling hand. Luther received the letter and instantly sent back the reply, "I command thee in the name of God to live. I still have need of thee in the work of reforming the church. . . . The Lord will never let me hear that thou art dead, but will permit thee to survive me. For this I am praying, this is my will, and may my will be done, because I seek only to glorify the name of God." These words may seem shocking to us, but one week later Myconius recovered. He died two months after the death of Luther in 1546.

There's a tension in all of this. It's easy to throw oneself on the sovereignty of God, but it's more exciting to wrestle. There's a tension between claiming God's power and grace and at the same time waiting on His will. However, this tension is not resolved by holding your persistence; it is resolved by accepting His answer.

B. "Watch in the same"

1. The basic meaning

Basically, the word *watch* means "to stay awake." It's difficult to pray when you're asleep. A good illustration of this meaning of the word *watch* is in Matthew 26:40-43. On the night of His betrayal Jesus brought His disciples with Him into the Garden of Gethsemane to pray. After He went off alone to pray, He came back, found the disciples asleep, and said to Peter, "What, could ye not watch [stay awake] with me one hour? Watch [stay awake] and pray, that ye enter not into temptation; the spirit indeed is willing, but the flesh is weak." In the gospels the word *watch* simply means "Don't go to sleep during prayer!"

2. The broad meaning

The meaning of "watch" in Colossians 4:2 is broader than merely staying awake. When Paul says, "Watch in the same," I believe he's referring to what Peter is saying in 1 Peter 4:7: "But the end of all things is at hand; be ye, therefore, sober minded, and watch unto prayer." In other words, look for the things that you ought to be praying about. If you're going to be consistent, if you're going to pour out your heart, and if you're going to really pray for something—then you ought to know what to pray for! You'll never be persistent with God about something you're not concerned about; and you'll never get concerned about something until you know what you need to be concerned about.

18

C. "With thanksgiving"

   1. Gratitude reflected in Colossians

    Verse 2 of chapter 4 is the fifth time in the book of Colossians that gratitude has been mentioned by Paul.

    a) Thankfulness for salvation (1:12)

    b) Thankfulness for spiritual growth (2:6)

    c) Thankfulness for fellowship with Christ and His Body (3:15)

    d) Thankfulness for the privilege to serve Him (3:17)

    e) Thankfulness for answered prayer (4:2)

   2. Gratitude reflected in us

    What should we be thankful for when we pray?

    a) For God's presence (Ps. 75:1)—If God weren't there, it wouldn't do us any good to pray. No matter what His answer might be—yes, no, maybe, wait—we should be thankful that He's listening.

    b) For God's provision (Acts 27:35)—God provides our food, shelter, and all the needs of our lives.

    c) For God's pardon (Rom. 6:17-18)—We used to be servants of sin; now we're servants of righteousness.

    d) For God's promise (1 Cor. 15:57; Rom. 8:28; 2 Cor. 2:14)—God promises us victory, that everything will work together for good and triumph. We can't lose in prayer. We may not get what we ask for, but we won't lose, because God knows that what He has for us is better than what we ask for.

No matter what the outcome of our prayers, we're to be thankful. Paul was saying, "I want you to pray—and when I say pray, I mean pray! Get in there and wrestle and persist with it.

Keep banging on the door until God gives you bread. Hold on till you're blessed."

The new man has a new mouth that has a new speech—the language of prayer.

Focusing on the Facts

1. Why is what comes out of our mouths so significant (see p. 8)?
2. True or false: Becoming a Christian will not necessarily change the way a person talks (see p. 8).
3. Why does the Bible emphasize controlling our speech (see p. 9)?
4. What is perhaps the truest indicator of a person's level of spiritual maturity (see p. 9)?
5. Describe some of the characteristics of the speech of unredeemed people (see pp. 9-11).
6. Describe some of the characteristics of the speech of redeemed people (see pp. 11-12).
7. Why is prayer so important? Be specific (see p. 13).
8. How often should we pray? Support your answer with Scripture (see p. 13).
9. What does it mean to be God-conscious (see p. 14)?
10. True or false: Since God knows what we need, there is no need to be persistent in prayer (see p. 14).
11. What does it mean to watch in prayer (Col. 4:2; see p. 18)?
12. Name some things we should express thanks for in our prayers (see p. 19).

Pondering the Principles

1. In this chapter we've seen characteristics of both redeemed and unredeemed speech. Look over the two lists. Do you find that some of the marks of unredeemed speech are also true of your speech? Are there some characteristics of redeemed speech you'd like to see more of in yourself? Pick some characteristics you'd like to work on this week, then memorize the verse given for them. Finally, tell your goal to another believer, and ask that person to hold you accountable to change.

2. In order to pray properly we must know what we are to pray for. One method for keeping alert in prayer is to use a prayer notebook. Keeping a list of prayer requests helps us remember what we should pray for, and a record of God's answers is an encouragement to our faith. You might wish to divide your notebook into different sections, such as family and friends, missionaries, your local church and its ministries, the people in your Bible study, the people you work with, and other divisions meaningful to you, and pray for one of those sections each day. If you do not already use a prayer notebook, why not begin this week? In time you'll have your own personal record of God's faithfulness to answer prayer.

2
The Speech of the New Man—Part 2

Outline

Introduction
A. Matthew 5:2
B. Luke 4:22
C. Luke 11:54
D. John 6:63
E. 1 Peter 2:22

Review
I. The Speech of Prayer (v. 2)

Lesson
II. The Speech of Proclamation (vv. 3-4)
   A. Paul's Imprisonment
      1. The occasion
      2. The opportunities
         a) Writing
         b) Evangelizing
         c) Proclaiming
            (1) Acts 21
            (2) Acts 24
            (3) Acts 26
            (4) Acts 28
   B. Paul's Prayer Request
      1. The plurality
      2. The parallel
      3. The petition
      4. The problem
         a) Moses (Ex. 4:10-13)
         b) Jeremiah (Jer. 1:6-9)

Introduction

One of the greatest Bible studies you could ever do would be to go through the New Testament and catalog everything Jesus said. Studying the speech of Jesus, we find, for example:

A. Matthew 5:2—"He opened his mouth and taught them." Jesus opened His mouth and instructed.

B. Luke 4:22—"All bore him witness and wondered at the gracious words which proceeded out of his mouth." Jesus opened His mouth and spoke graciously, gently, courteously, and becomingly.

C. Luke 11:54—The scribes and the Pharisees were "laying wait for him, and seeking to catch something out of his mouth, that they might accuse him." But they were never able to do it. Jesus never made an error with His mouth, which, according to James 3:2, shows that He was a perfect man.

D. John 6:63—In reference to the mouth of Jesus, this verse says, "The words that I speak unto you, they are spirit, and they are life."

24

E. 1 Peter 2:22—Peter said regarding the mouth of Jesus, "Who did no sin, neither was guile found in his mouth." Jesus never said a word that deceived anybody, tricked anybody, or covered up any truth.

In Colossians 4:2-6 Paul deals with four distinct elements in the speech of the new man.

Review

I. THE SPEECH OF PRAYER (v. 2; see pp. 13-19)

Lesson

II. THE SPEECH OF PROCLAMATION (vv. 3-4)

"Praying also for us, that God would open unto us a door of utterance, to speak the mystery of Christ, for which I am also in bonds; that I may make it manifest, as I ought to speak."

A. Paul's Imprisonment

1. The occasion

In Acts 21 Paul arrives in Jerusalem to give to the poor believers money that he has collected from all over the Gentile world. He also came to conciliate the Jews in the Jerusalem church with the Gentile believers. But shortly after he arrived chaos broke loose. "The Jews who were of Asia, when they saw him in the temple, stirred up all the people, and laid hands on him, crying out, Men of Israel, help! This is the man that teacheth all men everywhere against the people, and the law, and this place, and further brought Greeks also into the temple, and hath polluted this holy place. (For they had seen before with him in the city Trophimus, an Ephesian, whom they supposed that Paul had brought into the temple.) And all the city was moved, and the people ran together; and they took Paul, and drew him out of the temple,

25

and at once the doors were shut. And as they went about to kill him, tidings came unto the chief captain of the band, that all Jerusalem was in an uproar" (vv. 27-31).

Paul was taken as a prisoner by Roman soldiers but was finally delivered out of Jerusalem to Caesarea because of the Jewish plots to kill him (23:12-22). He was a prisoner in Caesarea for two years; and it was there that he gave his great speeches defending himself to Felix, Festus, and Agrippa. When he finally realized that he wasn't going to get anywhere with his appeals, he appealed to Rome and was sent there for trial. It was on this journey to Rome that he was shipwrecked (Acts 27). When he finally arrived in Rome, Acts 28:16 tells us that "Paul was permitted to dwell by himself with a soldier that kept him," and verse 30 tells us that he "dwelt two whole years in his own hired house, and received all that came unto him."

2. The opportunities

Paul's imprisonment proved to be a productive time for him. It was a time of:

a) Writing—It was during this time that Paul wrote Ephesians, Philippians, Colossians, and Philemon.

b) Evangelizing—Paul used his imprisonment as an opportunity to win soldiers in the Praetorian guard to Christ (cf. Phil. 1:13; 4:22).

c) Proclaiming—Acts 28:30-31 says that Paul spent his time "preaching the kingdom of God, and teaching those things which concern the Lord Jesus Christ, with all confidence, no man forbidding him." The time of his bondage was a time of proclamation.

(1) Acts 21—When Paul was first taken prisoner, he gave a sermon before the mob.

(2) Acts 24—Paul stood before Felix the governor and gave a great message.

(3) Acts 26—Paul stood before Herod Agrippa and gave another great message concerning the truth, including the wonderful testimony of his conversion.

(4) Acts 28—When he arrived as a prisoner in Rome, the first thing he did was to call all the Jews together so that he could evangelize them.

Everything was always an opportunity to Paul; he was always proclaiming. There were never any negative circumstances—only unique opportunities. Anyone who says, "Well, I'd like to do some proclaiming, but my circumstances don't permit it," is not being honest. It's not the circumstances that don't permit it, it's something else.

What did Paul ask the Colossians to pray for? Did he ask them to pray for his release from prison? No. He didn't care where his body was; he only wanted his mouth to have an effect wherever he was.

B. Paul's Prayer Request

1. The plurality

When Paul says "praying also for us" at the beginning of verse 3, he was probably including some of his friends and coworkers that were with him and mentioned at the end of this chapter.

2. The parallel

A similar prayer request is in Ephesians 6:19. In fact, the whole book of Ephesians is similar to Colossians. Ephesians 6:19 says, "[Pray] for me, that utterance may be given unto me, that I may open my mouth boldly to make known the mystery of the gospel, for which I am an ambassador in bonds; that in this I may speak boldly, as I ought to speak."

3. The petition

Paul didn't ask them to pray for his personal needs. He didn't say, "Pray for me that I'll hold up under stress," or, "Pray that I get released from prison." He in effect said, "Pray that I'll open my mouth and find a door for the Word—boldness!"

That actually isn't anything new. In the book of Acts, when the church was born, the first prayer meeting they ever had in which the events of the prayer meeting and their requests are recorded is described in Acts 4:29: "Now, Lord, behold their threatenings; and grant unto thy servants, that with all boldness they may speak thy word." And verse 31 says, "When they had prayed, the place was shaken where they were assembled together; and they were all filled with the Holy Spirit, and they spoke the word of God with boldness." The first known prayer of the early church was a prayer for utterance, boldness, and proclamation.

4. The problem

The mouth of the new man should speak the gospel; unfortunately, most Christians are like an arctic river —frozen over at the mouth! Somehow, because of inhibition or fear, we are lost to the effort of evangelism— unless we are continually prodded.

I know how Paul felt when he asked for the opportunity to speak the Word of God. What often arises is the fear that it can't be done in our own strength.

a) Moses (Ex. 4:10-13)—God said in effect to Moses, "Moses, speak for Me." And Moses said, "I can't—I stutter. What am I going to do?" And God said, "Who made your mouth?" In other words, "If I made it, I can make it work. Just trust Me!"

b) Jeremiah (Jer. 1:6-9)—When God told Jeremiah that he had been ordained a prophet, he said, "Ah, Lord God! Behold, I cannot speak." In other words, "If You think I'm going to get involved in this ministry

28

by myself, You've got another think coming." But God said to him, "Don't worry about it; I can do it through you."

That is what Paul is saying in Colossians 4:3. He's saying, "Look, I can't do it on my own. The Lord's going to have to provide a door for the Word."

5. The provision

God is the One in charge of providing open doors. What's a door? In the New Testament a door refers to an opportunity. In 1 Corinthians 16:9 and 2 Corinthians 2:12 God opens the door of opportunity for Paul to preach the Word. God closed the doors for Paul to go into Asia Minor and Bithynia (Acts 16:6-7), but then He opened the door for him to go into Macedonia (Acts 16:11-12). God opened and closed doors of opportunity for Paul—that's His business!

Paul said, "Just pray that God would give us an open door for the Word." That's all we need to pray—if we've got the courage to do it. Just pray for open doors, for opportunities. It takes a little courage to do that, because if you do, you're going to get the opportunities, and you're going to feel responsible for them. It's God's business to open doors.

a) Revelation 3:7-8—"To the angel of the church in Philadelphia write: These things saith he that is holy, he that is true, he that hath the key of David, he that openeth, and no man shutteth; and shutteth, and no man openeth." When the Lord shuts a door it's shut. When the Lord opens a door it's open. Verse 8 says, "I know thy works; behold I have set before thee an open door." God gave the church in Philadelphia an open door for the Word that nobody could shut. All He was asking was for them to proclaim it.

We have an open door in our country. There's no man that can forbid us to preach and no law to stop us. There's nothing to prevent it—except our own indolence, unfaithfulness, and self-will.

29

b) Acts 12:5-19—Herod had padlocked the prison doors and set a guard over Peter, but the Lord opened them because He wanted Peter to preach. The Lord opened literal doors to give him an open door to proclaim God's Word.

c) Acts 14:19-20—Paul was beaten and stoned at Lystra, but God sent him back into town, because He wanted him to preach. He returned to his brethren at Antioch and testified to the church there "all that God had done with them, and how he had opened the door of faith unto the Gentiles" (v. 27).

God has provided us with an open door. It's up to us to open our mouths and speak. The speech of the new man is a speech of proclamation.

C. Paul's Gospel

What is "the mystery of Christ" (v. 3)? It's the gospel and all that it embodies. It's all those sacred secrets hidden in the Old Testament and revealed in the New. It's all the truths about Jesus. For example:

1. The mystery of the indwelling Christ (Col. 1:26-27)—Christ indwells the believer.

2. The mystery of the incarnation (Col. 2:2-3)—Christ is God in human form.

3. The mystery of the rapture (1 Cor. 15:51-52)—Christ is going to return for His church.

4. The mystery of the bride (Eph. 5:23-32)—Christ has united Himself to us in an eternal way, as the bride and object of His love, to be consummated at "the marriage of the Lamb" (Rev. 19:7).

5. The mystery of iniquity (2 Thess. 2:7)—Christ is going to come and put an end to the fullness of sin.

6. The mystery of the church (Eph. 3:3-9)—Jew and Gentile are one in Christ (cf. Eph. 2:14-18).

D. Paul's Delivery

In verse 4 Paul states his goal: "That I may make it [the gospel] manifest, as I ought to speak." In Romans 1:14-15 Paul says, "I am debtor both to the Greeks and to the barbarians; both to the wise and to the unwise. So, as much as in me is, I am ready to preach the gospel." He was compelled to speak. In 1 Corinthians 9:16 he says, "Woe is unto me, if I preach not the gospel!" He didn't care about liberty for his feet, if he had liberty for his mouth. And he always wanted to speak the fullness of the mystery in the way that it ought to be done. God wants us to proclaim Christ, but He wants us to do it as it ought to be done.

I see two thoughts in the phrase "I ought to speak."

1. The importance of getting out there and sharing the gospel

2. The importance of sharing the gospel the right way

I'm afraid sometimes that a good message proclaimed in a bad way will do just about as much as a bad message. Paul wanted prayer about his own motivation and that he would speak the way he should speak about the gospel.

How Not to Present the Gospel

It's easy to present less than the full gospel and then ask people to commit their lives to something they don't even understand. In Acts 20:21 Paul, referring to how he preached, says, "Testifying [Gk., *diamarturomai*] . . . repentance toward God, and faith toward our Lord Jesus Christ." The word *diamarturomai* means "to give thorough and complete testimony about." In other words, Paul was saying, "I give thorough testimony—no half-baked evangelism."

I constantly warn pastors to avoid three types of evangelism:

1. Experience-centered evangelism—This is where you never actually preach the gospel but merely have somebody give the story of how his life was changed. One of the dangers in getting people to respond to a testimony rather than thorough information

about the gospel is that they don't know what they're responding to. They get "vaccinated," so that when somebody comes along later and says, "I want to tell you about Christ," they will say, "I tried that once, and it doesn't work."

2. Ego-centered evangelism—This approach asks, "How would you like this—and this—and this? Wouldn't you like this—and this—and this? Would this and this make you happy?" It's not fair to tell someone that if he receives Christ all his problems will be solved—because they won't be. In fact, I know people whose problems began when they became Christians. Don't promise people that; it isn't the gospel.

3. Expedience evangelism—This type of evangelism looks for a commitment from people—no matter how little they know. Make sure you don't present only part of the gospel to get them to make a commitment. Give them the whole message.

Don't work merely for a commitment; don't work merely to try to resolve people's problems; and don't try to get somebody hooked merely because you got hooked. Give them the truth in its totality so that they make an intelligent response to the total testimony concerning Christ.

III. THE SPEECH OF PERFORMANCE (v. 5)

"Walk in wisdom toward them that are outside, redeeming the time."

This departs from the mouth somewhat, but it is the most essential "speech" of all. The most important thing is not what you say; it's what you are. What you are gives credibility to what you say. The old saying "Your life speaks so loud, I can't hear what you're saying" is what Paul was talking about. Looking at verses 5-6 we see that "walk" comes before "talk." How are we to walk?

A. Walking in Wisdom

1. The character

What is wisdom? Wisdom properly evaluates circumstances and makes godly decisions. We are to walk with carefully planned, consistent, Christian life-styles. If you have any question about what walking in wisdom is read Ephesians 4-6.

2. The capacity

We have the capacity to walk in wisdom because we were given wisdom when we became Christians. Colossians 1:9-10 says, "For this cause we also, since the day we heard it, do not cease to pray for you, and to desire that ye might be filled with the knowledge of his will in all wisdom and spiritual understanding; that ye might walk worthy of the Lord unto all pleasing." We have already been saved and given wisdom; we now need to be filled with that wisdom that we might walk in it.

Do You Want to Be a Fool?

We've been given wisdom, but sometimes we turn our back on it and play the fool. In what ways can a Christian play the part of the fool?

1. Live for money (1 Tim. 6:9)—"But they that will be rich fall into temptation and a snare, and into many foolish and hurtful lusts."

2. Live legalistically (Gal. 3:1, 3)—"O foolish Galatians, who hath bewitched you, that ye should not obey the truth . . . ? Are ye so foolish? Having begun in the Spirit, are ye now made perfect by the flesh?"

3. Live with envy, strife, division, and confusion (James 3:13-16)—"Who is a wise man and endued with knowledge among you? Let him show out of a good life his works with meekness of wisdom. But if ye have bitter envying and strife in your hearts, glory not, and lie not against the truth. . . . For where envying and strife are, there is confusion and every evil work." That's foolish!

Four Ways to Acquire Wisdom

1. Reverence (Prov. 9:10)—"The fear of the Lord is the beginning of wisdom."

2. Prayer (James 1:5)—"If any of you lack wisdom, let him ask of God."

3. Study (Col. 2:2-3; 3:16)—"Christ, in whom are hidden all the treasures of wisdom and knowledge." If all wisdom exists in Christ, then, "Let the word of Christ dwell in you richly, in all wisdom."

4. Instruction (Col. 1:27-28)—"Christ in you, the hope of glory; whom we preach, warning every man, and teaching every man in all wisdom, that we may present every man perfect in Christ Jesus."

   3. The credibility

   When we "walk in wisdom toward them that are out-side," then what we say is going to mean something. How did the Colossians advertise their faith? The Colossians were a minority. They had no church building, no big cross, no billboards, no radio, no signs, no bumper stickers, no tracts, no books, no musical productions, no New Testaments—nothing. How did they get the message out? First they got the message in, then they lived it out. That was—and still is—the only credible message of evangelism in the world. Walk, then talk! I'm not against all those things I just mentioned, but all they do is confirm or deny the reality of Christianity that people read in the life of the Christians they know.

   Paul said, "Walk in wisdom toward them [non-Christians] that are outside."

B. Redeeming the Time

   The word *time* is not the Greek word *chronos*, from which we get "chronology" or "chronograph," which means time in terms of the clock. The Greek word used is *kairos*, which means time in terms of its opportunity. This phrase should

34

be translated "redeeming every opportunity." Psalm 90:12 says, "Teach us to number our days, that we may apply our hearts unto wisdom." It's a matter of buying opportunity.

Opportunity is short—it is here and gone. Life is short; people are dying. The Bible talks about the time coming when the door will be shut (Matt. 25:10), when "no man can work" (John 9:4), and when Jesus "will remove the candlestick" (Rev. 2:5). Romans 13:11-14 warns, "Knowing the time, that now it is high time to awake out of sleep. . . . The night is far spent, the day is at hand; let us, therefore, cast off the works of darkness, and let us put on the armor of light. Let us walk honestly, as in the day; not in reveling and drunkenness, not in immorality and wantonness, not in strife and envying. But put ye on the Lord Jesus Christ, and make not provision for the flesh, to fulfill its lusts."

When are you going to begin to live the way God wants? How much opportunity are you going to squander? When are you going to begin to tell that friend about Christ? When are you going to use those abilities and gifts God has given you?

Your walk talks. I hope it says the right thing to those on the outside. Every time you have an opportunity, redeem it. Purchase it for eternity. Life is short; it's foolish to waste it.

IV. THE SPEECH OF PERFECTION (v. 6)

"Let your speech be always with grace, seasoned with salt, that ye may know how ye ought to answer every man."

A. Speaking Graciously

Paul is not talking about the gospel as much as he is talking about general conversation. The mouth of a Christian should utter the speech of perfection. It should never utter lust, evil, deceit, cursing, oppression, lying, perversity, destruction, vanity, flattery, foolishness, babble, madness, verbosity, idle talk, false teaching, plotting, boasting, hatred, swearing, filthy talk, or gossip. Those are characteristics of an unregenerate person, not a Christian. Gracious

35

speech should be a habit whether you're being persecuted, whether you're in a stressful situation, whether you've been wronged, whether you're talking to your wife, husband, child, or neighbor. Whatever it is, let your speech be gracious.

What does it mean to speak graciously? It is referring to the speech that results from a heart changed by divine grace. However, that is not the primary idea in this passage. Primarily it means "to let your mouth speak what is spiritual, wholesome, fitting, kind, sensitive, purposeful, complimenting, gentle, truthful, loving, and thoughtful." It is not bitter, abrasive, vindictive, sarcastic, shady, angry, cutting, or boastful. Let your speech be gracious!

B. Speaking Pointedly

Salt prevents corruption. Our speech should act as a purifying, wholesome, cleansing influence, rescuing conversation from the filth that so often engulfs it (cf. Eph. 4:29). Let your speech be gentle, gracious, and thoughtful, but let it sting when it needs to. When there's a wound that needs to be healed, let it go right to the sore. And let it also be that which is pure and beautiful (the seasoning and flavor), rescuing conversations from corruption.

When the Greeks used the word *salt* in reference to speech they gave it the meaning of charm and wit. Wit is the ability to say just the right thing at the right time. Isn't that essentially what Paul is saying? "That ye may know how ye ought to answer every man." We are to have the right answer, for the right time, to the right person—that is the speech of perfection. Peter said, "Be ready always to give an answer to every man that asketh you a reason of the hope that is in you" (1 Pet. 3:15). Your mouth is important!

What comes out of your lips? Prayer? Proclamation? The speech of perfection? The right thing at the right time for the right person? That's the way the new man talks. If you're a Christian, you're a new man, and new speech should come along with your new life-style.

36

Do You Still Have the Smell of the Old Man?

The new man has a problem: even though he has become a new creature, his new nature has been so strongly influenced by the flesh that it's hard to discard it. Let me illustrate.

If you took a whiskey bottle and emptied it of all its contents, it would still stink—the old odor would remain. That is not unlike a Christian. You are a new creature, and the old contents are gone. However, some of the old odor is there. But if you pour into that whiskey bottle a fresh water supply, and then pour it out, continually repeating this process, little by little the smell will fade. When you become a Christian the old is poured out, but the smell is still there. As you're continually filled with the Spirit, cleansing will take place. And the more cleansing there is, the less scent there will be. The Holy Spirit takes over to remove the scent of our old life and to give our new life the fragrance of God.

We're new people, but we have an old scent. How is it going to be removed? Colossians 3 tells us that we are to "put off the old man with his deeds, and . . . put on the new man" (vv. 9-10). We are also to "let the peace of God rule" (v. 15), "let the word of Christ dwell" (v. 16), and let the name of Christ rule (v. 17). We are to take care how we live in the family with our wives, husbands, children, fathers, servants, and masters (3:18–4:1). And we are to take care of our mouths (4:2-6). If you take care of all those things in the energy of the Spirit of God, then the new man is going to be the man that God created him to be.

Focusing on the Facts

1. Name some of what characterized the speech of Jesus (see pp. 24-25).
2. How did Paul occupy his time during his imprisonment (see pp. 26-27)?
3. True or false: Our circumstances sometimes make it impossible for us to tell the gospel to others (see p. 27).
4. True or false: Paul pleaded with the Colossians to pray for his personal needs (see p. 28).
5. What is meant by the word *door* in Colossians 4:3 (see p. 29)?

6. Define "the mystery of Christ" (see p. 30).
7. Describe three types of evangelistic approaches to avoid (see pp. 31-32).
8. What you _____ gives credibility to what you _____ (see p. 32).
9. Define wisdom (see pp. 32-33).
10. Name three ways a Christian can act foolishly (see p. 33).
11. How can a person receive wisdom (see p. 34)?
12. What is graceful speech (see pp. 35-36)?
13. How should our speech resemble salt (see p. 36)?

Pondering the Principles

1. The apostle Paul was not a man who wasted time. Even in prison he made the best use of his time, writing several books of the New Testament and leading many to Christ. What about you? Are you "redeeming the time" (Col. 4:5)? Or are you too busy doing insignificant things to do what's most important? Here are a couple of suggestions to help you make better use of your time. First, make a list of the things you want to accomplish. Then go through your list and assign each item a priority. Do your high priority items first. Finally, use a daily planner to help you make the best use of your time each day.

2. One way to "walk in wisdom" (Col. 4:5) is to associate with wise people (Prov. 13:20). As we look at their lives, we can learn from their examples how to act wisely in different situations. We can also seek wise counsel from them when facing difficulties or decisions. The wise people God has placed in our lives are a blessing from Him. There is an additional source of wisdom available to us that we don't use as much as we should: many wise men and women of the past have left us a legacy in their writings and stories from their lives. By reading biographies of great figures in church history, we can learn from them how to walk in wisdom. By reading their writings, we can obtain their counsel on a wide range of subjects. If you can't remember the last time you read the biography of a wise person from years past, why not visit your church library or Christian bookstore today?

3
Taming the Tongue—Part 1

Outline

Introduction

Lesson
I. Its Potential to Condemn (vv. 1-2*a*)
  A. The Example of a Teacher
  B. The Definition of a Teacher
    1. Official teachers
      a) In the synagogue
      b) In the church
    2. Unofficial teachers
      a) In the synagogue
      b) In the church
  C. The Demands Made on a Teacher
    1. Caution
    2. Humility
    3. Seriousness
      a) Exemplified by Moses
      b) Exemplified by Ezekiel
      c) Exemplified by Paul
  D. The Dangers to a Teacher
    1. Bringing judgment upon himself
    2. Causing many to stumble
      a) James's warning
      b) Jesus' warning

II. Its Potential to Control (vv. 2b-5a)
   A. James's Emphasis
   B. James's Illustrations
      1. Bits used to control horses
      2. Rudders used to control ships

Conclusion

Introduction

James presents the issue of how we control our tongues as another test of living faith. The genuineness of a person's faith is demonstrated by his speech. The tongue is a great revealer of what is in the heart. James mentions speech in every chapter of his epistle (cf. 1:19, 26; 2:12; 4:11; 5:12), in keeping with his purpose in writing— to demonstrate that true believers, having been begotten by the Word of God (cf. 1:18), will manifest that new life in the way they live.

Throughout the first twelve verses of chapter 3, James personifies the tongue. Why didn't James refer to the heart instead of the tongue as the problem? Because the tongue reacts to what is in the heart. A common Jewish literary device was to attribute blame to a particular bodily part. For example, we read about "feet swift to shed blood" (Rom. 3:15) and the "eyes of adultery" (2 Pet. 2:14). We understand those verses as references to the guilt of the inner person. When James speaks of the mouth and the tongue, we understand them as the means by which the heart expresses itself.

Similarly, Paul focused on the tongue in characterizing the depravity and wretchedness of man. In Romans 3:13-14 he writes, "Their throat is an open sepulcher; with their tongues they have used deceit; the poison of asps is under their lips; whose mouth is full of cursing and bitterness." The mouth is the focal point of our fallenness and depravity.

Isaiah, overwhelmed by a vision of God's holiness, confessed his sinfulness by referring to himself as a man with a dirty mouth (Isa. 6:5). Nothing more vividly marks a man's sinfulness than his mouth.

The mouth is the monitor of the human condition. James tells us that right words are the manifestation of a righteous life. In chapter

3 he challenges us to measure our speech to see if it is consistent with our profession of faith. In so doing, he gives us five compelling reasons for controlling our tongues.

Lesson

I. ITS POTENTIAL TO CONDEMN (vv. 1-2*a*)

"My brethren, be not many teachers, knowing that we shall receive the greater judgment. For in many things we all stumble."

A. The Example of a Teacher

Those two verses speak of the judgment of those in teaching positions. Although James didn't mention the tongue here, the context is clearly the matter of speech. He warned his readers to take care not to thrust themselves into a teaching position, because a teacher has the potential to abuse his tongue and bring judgment upon himself. A faith that does not transform the tongue is not genuine saving faith—a point James makes clear in verse 26 of chapter 1: "If any man among you seem to be religious, and bridleth not his tongue, but deceiveth his own heart, this man's religion is vain." Since speech is a mark of true saving faith, it should be a proper measure of those who articulate and teach the faith.

By beginning with teachers, James points out that dead faith, hypocrisy, and deceit are dangers for all men, even those who are teachers in the church. They need to take a personal inventory of their speech to see if their faith is real. After introducing the subject at the level of teachers, James then moves to a more general discussion of everyone's speech.

Although verse 1 begins with the strong statement "Let not many become teachers," that does not mean God does not want His Word taught. In Numbers 11:29 Moses says, "Would God that all the Lord's people were prophets, and that the Lord would put his Spirit upon them!" There's a sense in which we wish everyone were a preacher or teacher, and indeed Matthew 28:19-20 calls us all to make disciples and teach all people. James does not deny that. Neither does he deny that there are some who are called to preach. Paul said, "Woe is unto me if I preach not the gospel!" (1 Cor. 9:16). In 1 Timothy 3:1 he commends those who desire to be elders—which primarily involves teaching. James doesn't want anyone to embark upon a teaching ministry without a sense of the seriousness involved. No doubt there were some in the assembly James was writing to who were becoming teachers with little or no thought about the implications.

James wanted to restrain his readers from rushing recklessly into the role of a teacher. Why? Because it is a much more serious matter to sin with your tongue in public than in private. Thus the potential for condemnation is far greater for a public speaker.

B. The Definition of a Teacher

1. Official teachers

The Greek word translated "teachers" is *didaskalos*. It is translated "master" in the gospels. James was talking about a person who is a teacher or preacher in an official capacity. James cautions against rushing into such official positions.

a) In the synagogue

In Jewish society the official teachers were known as rabbis. One example in the gospels is Nicodemus, who was recognized as a teacher in Israel (John 3:10). Some of them loved their title and the recognition, prestige, and power that went with it. It was easy for a rabbi to become the kind of person Jesus depicted as a spiritual tyrant, a seeker of the highest place at any function, a person who gloried in the respect shown him in public. The Lord strongly condemns that kind of attitude in Matthew 23:4-7. It is possible that some of James's readers had similar wrong motives.

42

b) In the church

The official teachers of the early church were known as apostles, prophets, pastors, evangelists, and teachers (1 Cor. 12:28; Eph. 4:11).

2. Unofficial teachers

a) In the synagogue

It was permissible in a synagogue for unofficial teachers to speak. Anyone who was respected and had reason to be heard could speak in a synagogue, even though he lacked formal schooling. Examples of that include the Lord Jesus Christ, who was a guest speaker in the synagogue at Nazareth (Luke 4:16-27), and Paul and Barnabas at Pisidian Antioch (Acts 13:14-15).

b) In the church

In 1 Corinthians 14:26 Paul writes, "When ye come together, every one of you hath a psalm, hath a doctrine, hath a tongue, hath a revelation, hath an interpretation. Let all things be done unto edifying." He then gives the Corinthians some guidelines to follow in their worship service. The early church included a format where the people in the congregation had the opportunity to give a teaching or a revelation.

There were official and unofficial teachers in both the synagogue and the church. James's statement is broad enough to encompass all who teach the Word of God.

C. The Demands Made on a Teacher

1. Caution

James urged caution for those who teach at any level, whether official or unofficial, because of the tremendous potential of the tongue to bring about condemnation. In a similar vein he wrote, "Wherefore, my beloved brethren, let every man be swift to hear, slow to speak" (1:19). The context of that verse indicates James was exhorting his readers to be swift to hear the Word of God and slow to speak it.

2. Humility

Many desire the prominence, authority, and honor that goes with the position of a teacher but give little or no thought to the responsibility of such a position. Paul refers to such people in 1 Timothy 1:6-7: "Some, having swerved, have turned aside unto vain jangling, desiring to be teachers of the law, understanding neither what they say, nor that about which they affirm." There were people like that at Ephesus, and no doubt also among those James wrote to—people who aspired to the role of teacher but were oblivious to the grave consequences of teaching error.

3. Seriousness

Although James was not seeking to discourage those genuinely qualified and called to teach, he nevertheless warned the prospective teacher to consider the seriousness of the position before assuming that role. He had in mind not only false teachers but also unqualified, unprepared, and wrongly instructed teachers.

a) Exemplified by Moses

Moses says to Aaron in Leviticus 10:3, "This is [what] the Lord spoke." That phrase sticks in my mind. There's one thing I continually ask of the Lord every time I speak, and it is, "Lord, please let me say what You intended to say." Teaching is a weighty responsibility. It is not to be embarked upon lightly.

b) Exemplified by Ezekiel

The responsibility of a teacher is given twice in the book of Ezekiel (3:17-18; 33:7-9). Ezekiel is pictured as a watchman at the city gate, responsible for warning the people of impending disaster. God said that if he failed to do so, their blood would be on his hands.

c) Exemplified by Paul

> Paul, almost with a sigh of relief, says in Acts 20:26-27, "I am pure from the blood of all men; I have not [failed] to declare unto you all the counsel of God." Paul had done his duty. Hebrews 13:17 says that leaders have to give an account to God for how they've led His people.

It is indeed a serious matter to be a teacher of God's Word. That is further confirmed by the terrifying judgment pronounced upon false teachers in passages such as 2 Peter 2 and the book of Jude. John Knox, the leader of the Reformation in Scotland, was overwhelmed by the seriousness of teaching God's Word. When asked publicly to take on the office and charge of preaching, he burst into tears, withdrew from the assembly, and did not appear again for days until he felt prepared.

James didn't want to warn others without including himself, so he writes in verse 1, "Knowing that we shall receive the greater judgment." By using "we" James included himself as one who was a teacher. All teachers are accountable to God for what they teach. That's why Paul commanded Timothy to be diligent in handling God's Word so that he wouldn't experience the shame of teaching error (2 Tim. 2:15). Paul said to be "nourished up in the words of faith and of good doctrine, unto which thou hast attained. But refuse profane and old wives' fables . . . give attendance to reading, to exhortation, to doctrine. . . . Meditate upon these things . . . take heed unto thyself and unto the doctrine" (1 Tim. 4:6-7, 13, 15-16). Teaching is an important matter.

D. The Dangers to a Teacher

1. Bringing judgment upon himself

The Greek word translated "judgment" (*krima*) is generally used in the New Testament to express a negative judgment. It is in the future tense, which implies that the judgment in view here is future judgment. For the unsaved false teacher it will be at the second coming of Christ. We read of that time in Jude 14-15: "The Lord cometh with ten thousands of His saints, to execute judgment upon all, and to convict all that are ungodly among them of all their ungodly deeds which they have ungodly committed, and of all their hard speeches which ungodly sinners have spoken against him."

The future judgment for believers is described in 1 Corinthians 4. We will stand face to face with Christ to receive whatever reward He deems fitting. Verse 5 says, "The Lord . . . will bring to light the hidden things of darkness, and will make manifest the counsels of the hearts; and then shall every man have praise of God." Earlier in that chapter Paul says he will wait until that time to have his ministry evaluated. It didn't matter what the Corinthians thought of his ministry—or what he himself thought—but only how God evaluated it (vv. 3-5). Paul ministered in light of that coming evaluation.

God Is the Audience

I've been asked on several occasions whom I prepare my sermons for. One reporter told me that the average newspaper is written on an eighth-grade level, then asked what level of listener I prepared my sermons for. I replied, "You might not understand this, but I prepare them for God. My only concern is that God be pleased, His name be honored, and His Word be treated fairly and honestly." And if I think I have done less than my best in preparing a sermon, I am miserable.

Being a teacher of God's Word is a dangerous occupation for anyone because of the power of the tongue to speak error, to speak inappropriately, or to misrepresent Christ. Even the apostle Paul was in a sense reluctant to preach God's Word, but he was compelled to (cf. 1 Cor. 9:16-17). And God was reluctant to allow him to preach until He took him out into the Arabian wilderness and trained him for several years (Gal. 1:17-18). Preaching is a weighty responsibility.

2. Causing many to stumble

   a) James's warning

James says in verse 2, "In many things we all stumble." Everyone sins in a myriad of ways. Proverbs 20:9 says, "Who can say, I have made my heart clean, I am pure from my sin?" The answer is no one. Second Chronicles 6:36 says, "There is no man who sinneth not." You can't put it any plainer than that. Paul says in Romans 3:23 that "all have sinned, and come short of the glory of God."

"Stumble" is used here as a synonym for the word *sin*. It means a moral lapse, a failure to do what is right, an offense against God. It is a present-tense verb in the Greek text. James is saying we all continually fail to do what is right—and the tongue is one significant way in which we fail.

Slips of the Tongue

The Bible has much to say about all the evil the tongue can cause. It refers directly or indirectly to a wicked tongue, a deceitful tongue, a lying tongue, a perverse tongue, a filthy tongue, a corrupt tongue, a bitter tongue, an angry tongue, a crafty tongue, a flattering tongue, a slanderous tongue, a gossiping tongue, a backbiting tongue, a blaspheming tongue, a foolish tongue, a boasting tongue, a murmuring tongue, a complaining tongue, a cursing tongue, a contentious tongue, a sensual tongue, a vile tongue, a tale-bearing tongue, a whispering tongue, and an exaggerating tongue. Do you find that any of those characteristics describe your tongue? No wonder God put our tongues in a cage behind our teeth, walled in by our mouths!

Most problems in life involve the tongue. Someone once said we should remember that the tongue is in a wet place and can slip easily. Nothing is more representative of man's sinfulness than his speech. There is no easier way to sin, because you can say anything you want. Circumstances may keep you from doing certain evil things, but you can say anything you choose.

b) Jesus' warning

In Matthew 12:34-37 Jesus is in an intense dialogue with the Pharisees, who accused Him of doing His miracles by the power of hell rather than heaven. He said to them, "O generation of vipers, how can ye, being evil, speak good things? For out of the abundance of the heart the mouth speaketh. A good man out of the good treasure of the heart bringeth forth good things, and an evil man out of the evil treasure bringeth forth evil things. But I say unto you that every idle word that men shall speak, they shall give account of it in the day of judgment. For by thy words thou shalt be justified, and by thy words thou shalt be condemned."

It's a sobering thought to realize a person's eternal destiny can be determined by his words. Although we are justified solely by faith in Jesus Christ, our justification will inevitably be made manifest in the words we speak. Words are a tattletale; they tell on the heart.

Gone But Not Forgotten

Have you ever wondered if the Lord keeps a record of everyone's words? It's easy for Him to do; He doesn't even have to write them down. I read a story some years ago about a man who turned on his television in London, England, and saw a half-hour program originating from Texas. He was so curious about the program that he called the station and found out it was a local broadcast made three years earlier! The only explanation that makes any sense about how he picked it up on his television is that once a broadcast goes out into the airwaves it stays there, and somehow it found its way to his set.

Scientists tell us the sound waves set in motion by every voice go on an endless journey through space. If we had instruments delicate and sophisticated enough, we could recapture those waves and recreate every word every person has ever spoken. God has such ability!

People will be judged on the basis of their words, because words are an accurate judge of the soul. A man's heart is his storehouse, and his words indicate what is stored there. Proverbs 15:28 says, "The mouth of the wicked poureth out evil things." When you give your life to Christ your tongue is transformed, and you have a new vocabulary. But even that new tongue can be a victim of old habits. James warns us to control the tongue because it has potential to condemn.

II. ITS POTENTIAL TO CONTROL (vv. 2b-5a)

"If any man offend not in word, the same is a perfect man, and able also to bridle the whole body. Behold, we put bits in the horses' mouths, that they may obey us; and we turn about their whole body. Behold also the ships, which, though they are so great and are driven by fierce winds, yet are they turned about with a very small helm, wherever the pilot willeth. Even so the tongue is a little member and boasteth great things."

A. James's Emphasis

There is some doubt about what James meant by "perfect" (Gk., *teleios*). It is possible he meant the perfection enjoyed by God. Someone who did not sin in his words would be perfect. If that is his meaning, he is saying no one is perfect, and so no one is immune to stumbling with his words.

On the other hand, he may be using the word *teleios* to express maturity. If a man does not continually stumble with his words, he is a spiritually mature man. It's impossible to be dogmatic about James's meaning here, but I lean toward the second view. James is saying only spiritually mature people can control their tongues. The only human being who had an absolutely perfect tongue was Jesus Christ, of whom it was said, "Never man spoke like this man" (John 7:46). His speech was perfect, absolutely without error. Peter, speaking of Christ, said He committed "no sin, neither was guile found in his mouth" (1 Pet. 2:22). Jesus did not sin in His actions or His words. To the degree that our holiness approaches the holiness of Christ, we are conformed to His image, and our speech will be godly.

James goes on to say in verse 2 that the one who doesn't sin with his speech is mature and "able also to bridle the whole body." That is a tremendously practical spiritual truth: if a person can master his tongue, he can control the rest of his evil tendencies as well. Since the tongue responds more quickly and easily to sin, if it were controlled the slower responding parts would also be controlled. If I want to bring my whole spiritual life under control, I ought to work on my tongue, because whatever spiritual dynamics work to control my tongue will work to control the rest of me. It makes it simple if we can concentrate only on the tongue. If the Holy Spirit gets control of the most volatile part of the body, the others will also be controlled. The psalmist puts it this way in Psalm 39:1: "I will guard my ways, that I may not sin with my tongue; I will guard my mouth as with a muzzle" (NASB).

B. James's Illustrations

1. Bits used to control horses

James says in verse 3, "Behold, we put bits in the horses' mouths, that they may obey us; and we turn about their whole body." You control a horse by controlling his tongue. You put a piece of metal in a horse's mouth. It lies on his tongue. Then you attach the reins to it, and when you pull on the reins, you pull the metal bit against the horse's tongue. By controlling a horse's tongue, you control its movements. Horses are useless without a bit. They don't voluntarily plow fields, pull wagons, or carry riders. You control the horse's body by putting a bit on its tongue. That illustrates James's point. If you get control of your tongue, you can direct your whole body. By controlling the tongue, one's whole life is directed to a useful purpose.

2. Rudders used to control ships

James gives another illustration in verse 4: "Behold also the ships, which, though they are so great and are driven by fierce winds, yet are they turned about with a very small [rudder], wherever the pilot willeth." How big were ships in biblical times? The one in Acts 27 was big enough to accommodate 276 people and a substantial amount of cargo. A small rudder directs a massive ship. The idea is this: power applied at the right point will control the whole vessel. Similarly, power applied at the right point in your life (your mouth) is sufficient to control the rest of you. James says to control your tongue because of its power to control you.

Speech Properly Seasoned

How do you control your tongue? By speaking only that which is gracious, kind, loving, true, thoughtful, holy, sensitive, edifying, gentle, comforting, humble, wise, unselfish, and peaceful. If you do that, you'll control every other part of your life, because the only way you can control your tongue is by being under the power of the Holy Spirit.

Conclusion

The tongue is like a master switch. In back of my house I have a panel with many circuit breakers. At the bottom is a master switch. You can switch off any circuit you want, or you can shut the whole thing down by throwing the master switch. Your tongue is the master switch that controls everything else in your life.

James sums up what he has been saying in verse 5: "The tongue is a little member and boasteth great things." The tongue is a braggart. James emphasized the power of the tongue. It can do great things. It is a powerful instrument. It can tear down people. It can tear down churches. It can destroy relationships. It can wreck a marriage. It can devastate a family. It can ruin a nation. It can lead to murder. It can lead to war. On the other hand, it can build up. It can minister love, enthusiasm, encouragement, comfort, peace, or joy. In light of that, James exhorts us to examine our speech. Is it consistent with genuine faith? We must control the tongue because of its power to condemn and control us.

Focusing on the Facts

1. In what way is our speech a test of the genuineness of our faith (see p. 40)?
2. What was James's purpose in writing his epistle (see p. 40)?

3. Why should a person be hesitant to become a teacher (see p. 41)?
4. Explain why James begins his discussion about speech with a reference to teachers (see p. 41).
5. True or false: Only duly accredited rabbis were permitted to speak in a Jewish synagogue (see p. 43).
6. True or false: Only the pastors and teachers were permitted to teach in the early church (see p. 43).
7. What judgment does James have in view in verse 1 (see pp. 45-46)?
8. What does it mean to stumble (v. 2; see p. 47)?
9. Why is it easier to sin with the mouth than in any other way (see p. 47)?
10. In what way will we be judged by our words (see p. 48)?
11. Describe two possible meanings for the Greek word translated "perfect" in verse 2 (see p. 49).

Pondering the Principles

1. The only person who never sinned in his speech was Jesus Christ. As Christians, we are to pattern our lives after His, including our speech. Choose one of the gospels and read through it this week, paying careful attention to the words the Lord spoke. Look for how He responded to His friends, His enemies, those who flattered Him, those who attacked Him, those who were self-righteous, and those who were hurting. Ask the Lord to show you where your speech fails to measure up to His example. Then commit yourself to work on changing those areas.

2. The book of Proverbs contains practical instruction on speech that honors God. Go through the list of sins of the tongue on page 47. Do you find yourself struggling with some of those sins? If so, use a concordance, topical Bible, or topical arrangement of the Proverbs and see if you can find a verse in Proverbs that speaks to your problem. Then memorize it. The next time you're tempted to say something you shouldn't, repeat your memory verse instead. By doing so you will train yourself to speak only that which is "good for edification according to the need of the moment" (Eph. 4:29, NASB).

4
Taming the Tongue—Part 2

Outline

Introduction
A. The Transformation of a Believer
1. His salvation
2. His sanctification
3. His speech
B. The Test of a Believer

Review
I. Its Potential to Condemn (vv. 1-2*a*)
II. Its Potential to Control (vv. 2*b*-5*a*)

Lesson
III. Its Potential to Corrupt (vv. 5*b*-6)
A. The Exclamation (v. 5*b*)
B. The Explanation (v. 6)
1. The tongue is a system of iniquity
2. The tongue defiles the body
3. The tongue infects the world around us
4. The tongue is fueled by hell
IV. Its Potential to Contend (vv. 7-8)
A. That Which Can Be Tamed (v. 7)
B. That Which Cannot Be Tamed (v. 8)
1. Explained
a) Psalm 140:3
b) Psalm 64:1-8
2. Exemplified
a) The sons of Laban
b) The princes of Ammon
c) The men of Jezreel

Introduction

Echoing through the halls of my childhood memories is a statement my mother frequently made: "Johnny, if I ever hear you say anything like that again, I'm going to wash your mouth out with soap!" I don't know if that technique is still being used by parents today, but I do know that there is less concern today over what is acceptable speech and what isn't. In our family, foul or unkind words were rare. As a result of my upbringing and my personal Christian beliefs, I have no tolerance for foul language.

James 3 offers the most definitive discussion of pure speech in the Bible. If James could speak to us today, he might emphasize the need for people to wash out their mouths spiritually. Also, the Lord was greatly concerned about this matter. Jesus taught that the heart is revealed in a person's speech and that an individual will be justified or condemned by his speech (Matt. 12:34-37). In other words, since your speech reveals the perspective of your heart, it can also determine your eternal destiny.

  A. The Transformation of a Believer

    1. His salvation

        The new birth of salvation (regeneration) with its attendant transformation (sanctification) makes you a new creation. Part of being a new creation is having new speech. Christians speak differently from other people.

What we say is not always perfect, but it is certainly different. In Colossians 3 the apostle Paul states the perspective that Christians should have: "If then you have been raised up with Christ, keep seeking the things above. . . . Set your mind on the things above, not on the things that are on the earth. For you have died and your life is hidden with Christ in God" (Col. 3:1-3, NASB).

2. His sanctification

Paul shows that when you become a new creation, you will have a whole new approach to life—a transformed nature will result in transformed behavior: "Consider the members of your earthly body as dead to immorality, impurity, passion, evil desire, and greed, which amounts to idolatry. For it is on account of these things that the wrath of God will come, and in them you also once walked, when you were living in them. But now you also, put them all aside: anger, wrath, malice, slander, and abusive speech from your mouth. Do not lie to one another, since you laid aside the old self with its evil practices, and have put on the new self who is being renewed to a true knowledge according to the image of the One who created him" (vv. 5-10, NASB).

3. His speech

A transformed heart leads to transformed speech. Verses 16-17 say, "Let the word of Christ richly dwell within you, with all wisdom teaching and admonishing one another with psalms and hymns and spiritual songs, singing with thankfulness in your hearts to God. And whatever you do in word or deed, do all in the name of the Lord Jesus, giving thanks through him to God the Father." Our speech is dramatically affected by our new nature.

B. The Test of a Believer

The tongue then serves as a test of the heart. James has already said, "If any man among you seem to be religious, and bridleth not his tongue, but deceiveth his own heart, this man's religion is vain [useless]" (James 1:26). Unless your salvation manifests itself in the way you speak, your salvation is nothing but self-deception. True faith will result in good works. One of the works that faith produces is speech that is honoring to God. True believers have a sanctified tongue not only as a sovereign reality but also as a duty to fulfill. That's the paradox of the Christian experience.

The Paradox of Divine Sovereignty and Christian Responsibility

Paradoxes are common in the Bible. For example, we are saved by sovereign grace, chosen before the foundation of the world, yet we have the responsibility to believe. Our salvation is secure by God's sovereign decree, yet we must persevere. We live by sovereign power because of Christ's living in us, yet we must obey. James describes believers as those who endure trials, obey Scripture, and do good to all people. However, the Christian has an obligation to consciously pursue those things. What God says will be true of us must be true of us. Just because God said it doesn't mean we can lie down flat on our backs and hope it happens. The paradox of God's providing and our producing is the result of divine regeneration and living faith. God produces good deeds and godliness through our commitment to obey.

When James speaks of the tongue he shows it reveals the condition of the heart, and at the same time he exhorts us to speak in a godly manner. So although this passage is a statement on the character of living faith as revealed by our speech, it is also a call for us to correct our speech, because the two go hand in hand.

Review

I. ITS POTENTIAL TO CONDEMN (vv. 1-2*a*; see pp. 41-49)

II. ITS POTENTIAL TO CONTROL (vv. 2*b*-5*a*; see pp. 49-51)

III. ITS POTENTIAL TO CORRUPT (vv. 5b-6)

A. The Exclamation (v. 5b)

"Behold, how great a matter a little fire kindleth!"

That verse is an exclamation of the tongue's potential for destruction. James obviously has in mind a great forest set aflame by a small fire. The potential impact of a small fire is staggering. One flame can set thousands of acres ablaze. Fire has an amazing capacity to multiply; water doesn't. If you pour out a cup of water, it won't become a flood. The tongue is like fire—what it says can set a whole town blazing. The imagery here is vivid because in the dry brush of Palestine, a small spark flying off of a fire could start a blaze that would cover the landscape, destroying everything in its path. The psalmist alluded to that when he prayed that God would destroy the wicked "as the fire burneth a forest, and as the flame setteth the mountains on fire" (Ps. 83:14).

B. The Explanation (v. 6)

"The tongue is a fire, a world of iniquity; so is the tongue among our members that it defileth the whole body, and setteth on fire the course of nature, and it is set on fire of hell."

Comparing the tongue to fire is common in Scripture. Proverbs 16:27 says, "An ungodly man diggeth up evil, and in his lips there is as a burning fire." Proverbs 26:20-21 says, "Where no wood is, there the fire goeth out; so where there is no tale bearer, the strife ceaseth. As coals are to burning coals, and wood to fire, so is a contentious man to kindle strife." One who engages in gossip, slander, or deceit adds fuel to the fire of strife and contention.

Verse 6 is one of the strongest statements ever made on the danger of speech. It describes the perilous nature of the tongue.

1. The tongue is a system of iniquity

   "World" (Gk., *cosmos*) in this context doesn't refer to the earth but to the world's evil system. James is saying that the tongue is a system of unrighteous expression within our human nature that rebels against God's standard. It is the focal point of behavioral unrighteousness within man. One commentator said it is the microcosm of evil among our members. No other bodily part has such far-reaching potential for disaster as the tongue.

2. The tongue defiles the body

   The tongue is one part of the body that can defile the entire person. It's like smoke from a fire, which permeates everything around it. When I was in college I bought a sport coat for nine dollars at a fire sale. Although it had smoke damage, I figured the smell would go away after a few days. But as long as I owned that coat (which wasn't long) I smelled like I was on fire, or at least like I was a heavy smoker! So the tongue is a raging fire whose smoke stains that which it doesn't consume. Our evil words stain our personalities like the smoke of a fire.

   The Greek word translated "defileth" means "to pollute." It is used in Jude 23: "Others save with fear, pulling them out of the fire, hating even the garment spotted [defiled] by the flesh." It refers to something that has been contaminated. A filthy tongue results in a filthy personality. Jesus said, "That which cometh out of the man, that defileth the man" (Mark 7:20).

3. The tongue infects the world around us

   Verse 6 says that the tongue "setteth on fire the course of nature." I believe a better translation is: "It is setting on fire the circle of life." James is showing the expanding influence of the tongue and carrying it beyond the individual to the people and circumstances in a person's life. The evil of the tongue stains not only you but everything you touch. Its effect encompasses your sphere of influence. People know you by how you talk. Gossip, rumors, slander, false accusations, lies, and evil speech destroy not only the reputation of a family, an organization, a school, a church, or a community, but also its ability to function properly.

4. The tongue is fueled by hell

The end of verse 6 says, "It is set on fire of hell." The Greek word translated "hell" is *gehenna,* which is used only in the four gospels with this one exception. The Lord used it to refer to the eternal place of burning where damned souls will go. He described it as a place "where their worm dieth not, and the fire is not quenched" (Mark 9:44). The tongue often becomes a tool of Satan to pollute our own lives and the lives of those we touch.

That is quite a description of the tongue's potential to corrupt. No wonder James was so concerned that we bring the tongue into control to the honor of God. David said the words of a traitor's "mouth were smoother than butter, but war was in his heart; his words were softer than oil, yet were they drawn swords" (Ps. 55:21). Sometimes the tongue is so subtle that we believe it means well when it intends evil. Every believer should realize that his tongue still has the power to devastate. Only in heaven will we have a glorified tongue that does nothing but praise God and speak righteousness.

IV. ITS POTENTIAL TO CONTEND (vv. 7-8)

A. That Which Can Be Tamed (v. 7)

"For every kind of beasts, and of birds, and of serpents, and of things in the sea, is tamed, and hath been tamed by mankind."

God gave man the authority to rule over the animal kingdom (Gen. 1:28). That fact was reiterated to Noah (Gen. 9:2-3). Man today still dominates the animal kingdom and is able to tame a variety of animals. If you've ever been to a circus, you've probably seen lions and tigers that allow the trainer to stick his head in their mouths. Maybe you've even seen people ride killer whales at an amusement park. Man is able to tame the wildest and fiercest of animals. The Greek word translated "kind" (*phusis*) means "nature."

James lists the basic classification of animals: those that walk, fly, crawl, and swim. Regardless of their classification, man is able to subdue wild animals.

B. That Which Cannot Be Tamed (v. 8)

"But the tongue can no man tame; it is an unruly evil, full of deadly poison."

1. Explained

However, no one can tame the tongue. Even with believers, the tongue breaks out of its cage. Notice that James doesn't say it can't be tamed; he merely says man can't tame it. There's a difference. Only God can tame it by His power. The first recorded sin after the Fall was an untamed tongue—Adam blamed God (Gen. 3:12). The first recorded miracle on the Day of Pentecost was the taming of the tongue in that men were enabled to proclaim the wonderful works of God in other languages (Acts 2:1-11).

James says the tongue is a savage beast. It's always lashing out, fighting against restraint. Furthermore, the tongue carries a deadly venom.

a) Psalm 140:3—"They have sharpened their tongues like a serpent; adders' poison is under their lips" (cf. Rom. 3:13).

b) Psalm 64:1-8—"Hear my voice, O God, in my prayer; preserve my life from fear of the enemy. Hide me from the secret counsel of the wicked, from the insurrection of the workers of iniquity, who whet [sharpen] their tongue like a sword, who bend their bows to shoot their arrows, even bitter words, that they may shoot in secret at the perfect [the righteous ones]. Suddenly do they shoot at him, and fear not. They encourage themselves in an evil matter; they speak of laying snares secretly; they say, Who shall see them? They search out iniquities; they accomplish a diligent search. Both the inward thought of every one of them, and the heart, are deep. But God shall shoot at them with an arrow; suddenly shall they be wounded. So they shall make their own tongue to fall upon themselves; all that see them shall flee away." The psalmist conveys the destructiveness of the tongue.

2. Exemplified

a) The sons of Laban

Laban's sons spoke ill of Jacob before their father (Gen. 31). That resulted in Jacob's secretly fleeing from Laban's home.

b) The princes of Ammon

Some princes of Ammon falsely accused David of deceit in his attempt to honor their new king (Hanun) and his father (Nahash), who recently had died. As a result Hanun humiliated David's servants and hired a Syrian army to protect himself against retaliation. Those measures escalated into a battle in which the Syrians lost seven hundred charioteers and forty thousand horsemen along with their commander (1 Chron. 19:18).

c) The men of Jezreel

When Naboth the Jezreelite refused to give up his vineyard to the vile King Ahab of Samaria, Ahab's wife, Jezebel, arranged to have Naboth falsely accused of blasphemy and stoned. She encouraged the leaders of the city to hold a feast at which Naboth was to be the guest of honor. However, two worthless men were enlisted to accuse Naboth in the middle of the feast and bring about his demise so Ahab could acquire the vineyard. Pretense and slander eventually resulted in the murder of Naboth and the devastation of Ahab and his posterity, as well as the death of Jezebel, whose body was eaten by mongrel dogs in the street (1 Kings 21:1-24).

d) The advisers of Zedekiah

The princes of Judah spoke evil of the prophet Jeremiah and persuaded King Zedekiah to imprison him. The king allowed them to throw Jeremiah into a dungeon where he sunk in the mire (Jer. 38).

e) The contemporaries of Christ

The Jewish leaders accused the greatest prophet, John the Baptist, of being demon possessed. They referred to the spotless Son of God as being a glutton, a drunkard, and a friend of outcasts and sinners (Matt. 11:18-19).

Many people have died because of the deadly poison of the tongue. The Lord was crucified after being falsely accused (Luke 23:2, 20-25). Those who despised the gospel secretly induced men to lie about Stephen and accuse him of blasphemy. They succeeded in stirring up the people with their words, and Stephen was stoned to death (Acts 6:9-14; 7:57-60).

When Paul arrived in Jerusalem in Acts 21, Jews from Asia stirred up the people against him, falsely accusing him of bringing a Gentile in the Temple. They dragged Paul out to kill him, but the Roman guard intervened. That controversy resulted in Paul's spending the next several years under arrest.

The tongue can be a deadly poison, destroying reputations and even life in its wake.

V. ITS POTENTIAL TO COMPROMISE (vv. 9-12)

A. Conveyed (v. 9)

1. In blessing (v. 9*a*)

"Therewith bless we God, even the Father."

"Therewith" refers to the tongue. The tongue can be used to bless God, one of its most wonderful functions.

James's Jewish readers would have readily identified with such a statement since it was Jewish tradition to follow the mention of God's name with the phrase "blessed be He." Also, three times a day devout Jews repeated eighteen benedictions that ended with "blessed be Thou, O God." It was customary for Jewish people to bless God throughout the day. The psalms are full of such blessings (Ps. 68:19, 35; 136).

2. In cursing (v. 9*b*)

"Therewith curse we men, who are made after the similitude [likeness] of God."

There is the duplicity and hypocrisy of the tongue. The same tongue that blesses God frequently curses those made in His image. Out of the mouth comes slander, criticism, anger, jealousy, envy, and bitterness. To curse is to wish evil on someone. It is tragic that we curse what was made in the likeness of God. Although that likeness has been marred, it is still recognizable in the rational, personal, and moral nature of man. Like God, man can know, love, and act on the basis of rational thought and motive. James was saying it is inconsistent that we would praise God and then turn around and criticize His creation, especially that which was made in His image.

B. Condemned (v. 10)

"Out of the same mouth proceed blessing and cursing. My brethren, these things ought not so to be."

Scripture provides many illustrations of people blessing and cursing simultaneously. The Pharisees in one breath blessed God and cursed Christ (Matt. 26:63-68). The apostle Peter said, "Thou art the Christ, the Son of the living God" (Matt. 16:16), and a few weeks later he cursed venomously, "I know not the man" (Matt. 26:74). The apostle Paul gave an impressive defense and testimony in Acts 22 but then cursed the high priest with words that have no place in the mouth of a servant of God: "God shall smite thee, thou whited wall" (23:3; cf. John 18:19-23).

The strong negative translated "ought not" (Gk., *ou chrē*) is used only here in the entire New Testament. Profane speech is inconsistent and unacceptable for the believer— it's a compromise of our potential and God's standard. God saved us and transformed us, giving us a capacity for new speech. Therefore He expects us to speak in a manner that is honoring to others and Him.

C. Compared (vv. 11-12)

James illustrates the inappropriateness of cursing by three examples from nature.

1. To spring water (v. 11)

   "Doth a fountain send forth at the same place sweet water and bitter?"

   The answer to that rhetorical question is no. The use of the Greek word *mēti* in a question shows that James expects a negative answer. The Greek verb translated "send out" means "to burst forth" or "to gush." The same opening in the ground or source of a spring produces water that's either drinkable or not drinkable —but not both.

2. To vegetation (v. 12*a*)

   "Can the fig tree, my brethren, bear olive berries? Either a vine, figs?"

   It is impossible for olives to grow on a fig tree or for figs to grow on a grapevine. Simple observation teaches us that each kind of vine or tree will produce only the fruit that is in harmony with its nature.

3. To salt water (v. 12*b*)

   "So can no fountain yield both salt water and fresh."

   That is a conclusion, not a question. Just as one would not expect to go to the Dead Sea and find fresh water, we should not expect one who has a clean heart to pronounce unwholesome words. The taste of the product reveals the nature of its source, and likewise the speech of a person reveals whether he has a heart of faith. If a person is a true believer, his speech should give evidence of that fact rather than contradict it.

Although once in a while you may find some bitter water among fresh, keep in mind that James is speaking in general terms. Even in the speech of Christians exceptions may be found, but a transformed life will generally produce transformed words. Critical words come from a critical heart. Defamatory, unloving speech issues from a heart where the love of Jesus is absent. True believers will be revealed by their speech.

Conclusion

James presents the tension between what the believer ought to be and what he must strive to be. It's the tension of being positionally righteous in Christ but falling short of that position in our daily lives. So although it is true that a Christian's speech will be consistent with his new nature and God's holy purposes, he has the obligation to make sure that is true in his own life.

In Luke 6:43-45 Jesus says, "A good tree bringeth not forth corrupt fruit; neither doth a corrupt tree bring forth good fruit. For every tree is known by its own fruit. For from thorns men do not gather figs, nor from a bramble bush gather they grapes. A good man, out of the good treasure of his heart, bringeth forth what is good; and an evil man, out of the evil treasure of his heart, bringeth forth that which is evil; for of the abundance of the heart his mouth speaketh." I believe James had this passage in mind when he wrote that.

The true believer is known by his speech—his tongue is under control. Peter says he who desires to "love life, and see good days [should] . . . refrain his tongue from evil, and his lips that they speak no [deceit]" (1 Pet. 3:10). James warned us that our spiritual life and maturity are revealed by our words and that the tongue has tremendous potential for disaster. Therefore he calls us to tame it. If we do, it's evidence that we are walking in obedience.

Examine your life. If you hear words coming out of your mouth that ought not to, you need to confess your sin to God and turn from it.

How you react to those times when bitter water comes out of what is to be a sweet fountain is the key to your spiritual strength.

Focusing on the Facts

1. What is the most definitive discussion of pure speech in all the Bible (see p. 54)?
2. By what did Jesus say a person would be justified or condemned? Why (Matt. 12:34-37; see p. 54)?
3. When a person becomes a new creation in Christ, what does his transformed nature result in (see p. 55)?
4. The tongue serves as a test of _____. Explain (see p. 55).
5. Identify some common paradoxes in the Bible (see p. 56).
6. Does God's saying that certain qualities will be true of Christians mean that we need not expend any effort in pursuing those qualities? Explain (see p. 56).
7. Explain why the tongue is like a fire (see p. 57).
8. How far-reaching is the influence of the tongue (see pp. 58-59)?
9. Who influences us to make evil use of the tongue (see p. 59)?
10. When will we have tongues that do nothing but praise God and speak righteousness (see p. 59)?
11. According to verse 7 what does man have the ability to tame (see p. 59)?
12. Is it possible for the tongue to be tamed? How (see p. 60)?
13. The psalmist of Psalm 64 likened the tongue to _____ (see p. 60).
14. Give some examples of people in Scripture who were victimized by the tongue (see pp. 61-62).
15. We use our tongues for what good purpose (see p. 62)?
16. What hypocrisy is the tongue capable of, according to verse 9 (see p. 63)?
17. Cite the incidents of blessing and cursing that came out of Peter's mouth (Matt. 16:16; 26:74; see p. 63).
18. What conclusion can we draw from James's illustrations from nature in verses 11-12 (see pp. 64-65)?
19. Explain the tension that James presents (see p. 65).

Pondering the Principles

1. The issue of what God has done for us and what we must do ourselves can be confusing. Because of the goodness of God and the sinfulness of man we should be quick to credit God with our successes and to accept responsibility for our failures. Do you have a problem maintaining wholesome speech? Do you find it easy to blame your work environment or your up-bringing for the language you use? Meditate on Colossians 3:1-17, noting the things that God has done for us and the things Paul encourages us to do. Commit yourself today to making not only your speech but all areas of your spiritual growth your re-sponsibility as you actively cooperate with the Holy Spirit.

2. If a stranger were to hear everything you said on a good day as well as a bad day, do you think he would see any consistency in the wholesomeness of your words and conclude that your speech is under control? Or do you think that your words would reveal a discrepancy between what you believe and what you actually say and do? Jesus said that "the good man out of the good trea-sure of his heart brings forth what is good . . . for his mouth speaks from that which fills his heart" (Luke 6:45, NASB). What fills your heart—worldly wisdom, materialistic goals, self-indul-gence? Or is it the wisdom of God's Word, the desire to be more like Christ, and a commitment to serve others? Make sure you are consistently filling your heart with the treasure of God's Word so that His desires and goals can become yours. Then your life-style and your speech will reflect the control of the Spirit in your life.

Scripture Index

Topical Index

Moody Press, a ministry of the Moody Bible Institute, is designed for education, evangelization, and edification. If we may assist you in knowing more about Christ and the Christian life, please write us without obligation: Moody Press, c/o MLM, Chicago, Illinois 60610.